QUICK CARDS
for
MENTAL MATHS

Number Operations

by
Robert Thompson

A QEd Publication

Published in 2004

© Robert Thompson

ISBN 1 898873 36 4

Published by QEd, The Rom Building, Eastern Avenue, Lichfield, Staffs. WS13 6RN
Web site: www.qed.uk.com
Email: orders@qed.uk.com

Printed in the United Kingdom by Stowes (Stoke-on-Trent).

Contents

Introduction

Quick Cards for Mental Maths are designed to be used by pairs of children or an adult with a child. Very simply, the cards have a question on one side and the solution on the reverse. One child (or adult) holds a card up for another to answer and then looks at the solution to check if it is correct.

The intention behind *Quick Cards* is to provide children with the opportunity of reinforcing addition, subtraction, multiplication and division skills in a way that they enjoy. It is also an excellent way of doing mental mathematics. Tried and tested in the classroom, these activities consistently receive a favourable response from children.

The cards have proved to be a very useful tool when working with children with special educational needs. Similarly, with children who love being tested you can set challenging tasks, such as 'How many cards can you answer correctly in three or four minutes?'

The advantage of *Quick Cards* is that the activity can be carried out independently by pairs of children. Pupils get immediate feedback on their responses. They can be made available for pupils to work on during spare moments or even wet lunchtimes. As far as the teacher is concerned no preparation and no marking are required.

The obvious disadvantage is that the activity is pupil-monitored and the teacher may have difficulty checking the progress that children are making.

Photocopying

The pages have been laid out in such a way as to enable you to photocopy the sheets back-to-back and then cut the cards out. When photocopying make sure you copy the page correctly so that the answers correspond to the questions! We have produced it in such a way to enable you to cut the cards directly from the pages in the book if you wish.

Doubles and near doubles within 20

This is a set of 24 cards which allows pupils to practise adding doubles and near doubles.

$3p + 2p$

$7 + 7$

$9 + 10$

$1 + 1$

$8p + 7p$

$5 + 6$

$1 + 0$

$8p + 8p$

14

5p

2

19

11

15p

16p

1

$$2 + 1$$

$$2 + 2$$

$$9p + 8p$$

$$3p + 3p$$

$$9 + 9$$

$$6p + 7p$$

$$6 + 6$$

$$3 + 4$$

4

3

6p

17p

13p

18

7

12

8 + 9

7 + 8

4p + 3p

5p + 5p

10 + 9

7 + 6

4p + 4p

10 + 10

15

17

10p

7p

13

19

20

8p

Addition within 20

This is a set of 24 cards which allows pupils to practise adding two numbers where the total does not exceed 20.

$$9 + 4$$

$$7 + 4$$

$$11 + 8$$

$$10 + 6$$

$$12 + 6$$

$$6 + 8$$

$$15 + 3$$

$$8 + 3$$

11   13

16   19

14   18

11   18

13 + 6

16 + 4

8 + 5

13 + 4

7 + 5

7 + 12

5 + 9

4 + 14

20

19

17

13

19

12

18

14

$$9 + 6$$

$$5 + 11$$

$$7 + 9$$

$$14 + 5$$

$$17 + 3$$

$$9 + 3$$

$$11 + 9$$

$$4 + 8$$

16

15

19

16

12

20

12

20

Subtraction facts within 20

This is a set of 24 cards which allows pupils to practise all subtraction facts within 10 and some of the easier subtraction facts within 20.

$$9 - 4$$

$$10 - 5$$

$$11 - 2$$

$$10 - 8$$

$$12 - 2$$

$$13 - 10$$

$$9 - 3$$

$$9 - 6$$

5   **5**

2   **9**

3   **10**

3   **6**

19 - 2

7 - 4

17 - 1

8 - 5

10 - 2

11 - 1

7 - 3

18 - 10

3

17

3

16

10

8

8

4

8 - 4

9 - 8

14 - 1

6 - 3

9 - 5

16 - 10

8 - 3

10 - 4

1

4

3

13

6

4

6

5

Doubling and halving

This is a set of 32 cards which allows pupils to practise doubling numbers to 20, doubling multiples of 10 to 100, halving even numbers to 20 and halving multiples of 10 to 100.

Double 4

Double 70

Double 15

Double 50

Double 3

Double 11

Double 13

Double 90

140

8

100

30

22

6

180

26

Double 18

Double 60

Double 9

Double 40

Double 14

Double 19

Double 5

Double 17

120

36

80

18

38

28

34

10

Half of 80	Half of 20
Half of 32	Half of 22
Half of 14	Half of 200
Half of 10	Half of 70

10

40

11

16

100

7

35

5

Half of 28

Half of 60

Half of 50

Half of 16

Half of 40

Half of 100

Half of 24

Half of 30

30

14

8

25

50

20

15

12

Multiplication to 10 X 10

This is a set of 32 cards which allows pupils to practise multiplication facts up to 10 X 10.

9×8

5×4

0×7

8×3

7×6

4×2

9×9

6×1

20

72

24

0

8

42

6

81

7 x 3

4 x 9

6 x 5

7 x 9

1 x 8

7 x 7

8 x 5

10 x 7

36

21

63

30

49

8

70

40

4 x 6	4 x 8
5 x 3	8 x 7
2 x 6	9 x 5
4 x 7	2 x 8

32   **24**

56   **15**

45   **12**

16   **28**

4 × 3

8 × 8

6 × 3

6 × 9

7 × 5

6 × 8

6 × 6

10 × 8

64

12

54

18

48

35

80

36

Division with no remainders

This is a set of 32 cards which allows pupils to practise division facts within 100. There are no remainders in the answers.

$72 \div 8$	$20 \div 4$
$18 \div 9$	$24 \div 3$
$42 \div 6$	$8 \div 2$
$81 \div 9$	$6 \div 1$

5   9

8   2

4   7

6   9

$$21 \div 3$$

$$36 \div 9$$

$$30 \div 5$$

$$63 \div 9$$

$$8 \div 8$$

$$49 \div 7$$

$$40 \div 5$$

$$70 \div 7$$

4   7

7   6

7   1

10   8

$$24 \div 6$$

$$32 \div 8$$

$$15 \div 3$$

$$56 \div 7$$

$$12 \div 6$$

$$45 \div 5$$

$$28 \div 7$$

$$16 \div 8$$

4

4

8

5

9

2

2

4

$$12 \div 3$$

$$64 \div 8$$

$$18 \div 3$$

$$54 \div 9$$

$$35 \div 5$$

$$48 \div 8$$

$$36 \div 6$$

$$80 \div 8$$

8

4

6

6

6

7

10

6

Division with remainders

This is a set of 32 cards which allows pupils to divide a two digit number by a single digit number using known multiplication facts within 10 X 10.

$$41 \div 5$$

$$26 \div 3$$

$$57 \div 6$$

$$43 \div 8$$

$$76 \div 10$$

$$38 \div 9$$

$$29 \div 5$$

$$77 \div 8$$

8 rem 2

8 rem 1

5 rem 3

9 rem 3

4 rem 2

7 rem 6

9 rem 5

5 rem 4

$26 \div 7$

$20 \div 3$

$60 \div 9$

$17 \div 2$

$10 \div 4$

$48 \div 7$

$29 \div 8$

$17 \div 6$

6 rem 2

3 rem 5

8 rem 1

6 rem 6

6 rem 6

2 rem 2

2 rem 5

3 rem 5

$$37 \div 4$$

$$13 \div 3$$

$$28 \div 6$$

$$24 \div 9$$

$$9 \div 2$$

$$33 \div 5$$

$$53 \div 10$$

$$18 \div 4$$

4 rem 1   9 rem 1

2 rem 6   4 rem 4

6 rem 3   4 rem 1

4 rem 2   5 rem 3

$$11 \div 7$$

$$76 \div 9$$

$$16 \div 5$$

$$8 \div 3$$

$$62 \div 8$$

$$32 \div 6$$

$$23 \div 4$$

$$50 \div 7$$

8 rem 4   1 rem 4

2 rem 2   3 rem 1

5 rem 2   7 rem 6

7 rem 1   5 rem 3

Subtract single digit from multiple of 100

This is a set of 32 cards which allows pupils to practise subtracting a single digit from a 3-digit multiple of 100.

200 - 4	200 - 6
200 - 9	200 - 3
900 - 8	300 - 4
300 - 1	300 - 5

194

196

197

191

296

892

295

299

300 - 2

900 - 7

400 - 5

400 - 8

400 - 1

400 - 3

900 - 6

500 - 5

893   298

392   395

397   399

495   894

500 - 9

500 - 4

500 - 2

900 - 3

600 - 2

600 - 7

600 - 4

600 - 6

496   491

897   498

593   598

594   596

700 - 8

700 - 3

700 - 5

700 - 1

800 - 2

800 - 4

800 - 8

800 - 9

697   692

699   695

796   798

791   792

Subtract 1 digit from 3 digit number bridging the hundred

This is a set of 32 cards which allows pupils to practise subtracting a single digit from a 3 digit number bridging the hundred.

202 - 4	205 - 6
207 - 9	201 - 8
304 - 8	303 - 4
303 - 7	301 - 5

199

198

193

198

299

296

296

296

401 - 2	402 - 7
403 - 5	405 - 8
505 - 9	503 - 4
502 - 6	503 - 5

395   399

397   398

499   496

498   496

606 - 9	603 - 4
604 - 7	601 - 3
703 - 4	704 - 7
702 - 4	703 - 6

599

597

598

597

697

699

697

698

Subtract 1 digit from 3 digit number bridging the hundred   Sheet 4

805 - 8

801 - 3

803 - 5

804 - 9

903 - 5

901 - 4

906 - 8

902 - 9

78

798   797

795   798

897   898

893   898

Subtract single digit from multiple of 1000

This is a set of 32 cards which allows pupils to practise subtracting a single digit from a 4 digit multiple of 1000.

2000 - 4	2000 - 6
2000 - 9	2000 - 3
3000 - 8	3000 - 4
3000 - 1	3000 - 5

1994   1996

1997   1991

2996   2992

2995   2999

4000 - 2	4000 - 7
4000 - 5	4000 - 8
5000 - 1	5000 - 3
5000 - 6	5000 - 5

3993　　　**3998**

3992　　　**3995**

4997　　　**4999**

4995　　　**4994**

6000 - 9	6000 - 4
6000 - 2	6000 - 3
7000 - 2	7000 - 7
7000 - 4	7000 - 6

5996   5991

5997   5998

6993   6998

6994   6996

8000 - 8

8000 - 3

8000 - 5

8000 - 1

9000 - 2

9000 - 4

9000 - 8

9000 - 9

7997   7992

7999   7995

8996   8998

8991   8992

Adding decimals - whole number answer

This is a set of 32 cards which allows pupils to practise adding two decimal numbers containing units and tenths where the total is a whole number.

Adding decimals - whole number answer   Sheet 1

2.6 + 8.4	9.3 + 7.7
6.9 + 8.1	1.5 + 8.5
4.8 + 8.2	9.7 + 9.3
5.2 + 7.8	3.4 + 2.6

17　　　　　　**11**

10　　　　　　**15**

19　　　　　　**13**

6　　　　　　**13**

8.7 + 6.3

4.5 + 8.5

1.6 + 1.4

3.2 + 4.8

9.9 + 8.1

7.6 + 4.4

8.3 + 2.7

5.5 + 6.5

13

15

8

3

12

18

12

11

$0.4 + 2.6$

$3.9 + 7.1$

$2.3 + 2.7$

$5.9 + 8.1$

$6.6 + 7.4$

$1.8 + 8.2$

$3.5 + 4.5$

$5.2 + 9.8$

11

3

14

5

10

14

15

8

9.6 + 9.4

2.7 + 1.3

8.8 + 2.2

3.1 + 9.9

6.4 + 4.6

9.3 + 7.7

4.2 + 6.8

9.2 + 8.8

4

19

13

11

17

11

18

11

Adding decimals - units and tenths

This is a set of 32 cards which allows pupils to practise adding decimals where both numbers contain units and tenths and where bridging may or may not occur.

$$2.6 + 8.8$$

$$9.1 + 7.7$$

$$6.9 + 8.7$$

$$1.6 + 8.5$$

$$4.8 + 8.9$$

$$9.5 + 9.3$$

$$5.2 + 7.4$$

$$3.4 + 2.7$$

16.8   11.4

10.1   15.6

18.8   13.7

6.1   12.6

Adding decimals - units and tenths

8.7 + 6.6

4.4 + 8.5

1.6 + 1.8

3.7 + 4.8

9.2 + 8.1

7.8 + 4.4

8.3 + 2.1

5.5 + 6.9

12.9   15.3

8.5   3.4

12.2   17.3

12.4   10.4

0.8 + 2.6	3.9 + 7.2
2.5 + 2.7	5.9 + 8.9
6.6 + 7.7	1.6 + 8.2
3.1 + 4.5	5.5 + 9.8

11.1   3.4

14.8   5.2

9.8   14.3

15.3   7.6

$$9.6 + 9.8$$

$$2.1 + 1.3$$

$$8.8 + 2.6$$

$$3.7 + 9.9$$

$$6.4 + 4.2$$

$$9.3 + 7.5$$

$$4.7 + 6.8$$

$$9.3 + 8.8$$

3.4

19.4

13.6

11.4

16.8

10.6

18.1

11.5